Original title:
Rising Strong

Copyright © 2024 Swan Charm
All rights reserved.

Author: Olivia Orav
ISBN HARDBACK: 978-9916-79-167-7
ISBN PAPERBACK: 978-9916-79-168-4
ISBN EBOOK: 978-9916-79-169-1

The Divine Embrace of Struggle

In shadows deep, where trials loom,
Faith ignites, dispelling gloom.
Each heartbeat sings a sacred thought,
In every pain, a lesson sought.

Mountains rise and rivers bend,
In struggle's hold, we find a friend.
With every fall, the Spirit calls,
To rise anew, as darkness falls.

Hands uplifted, spirits soar,
In sacred strife, we learn the lore.
The heart rejoices, the soul arrays,
In every struggle, hope displays.

Through storms of doubt and waves of fear,
The quiet strength, forever near.
Each tear a seed, each scar a hymn,
In toil we find the love within.

The journey's path is etched in light,
With every step, we share the fight.
Together we rise, our spirits blend,
In divine embrace, we learn to mend.

Trust in the Divine Plan

In shadows deep, the light shines clear,
A path unfolds, with hope held dear.
With faith as our guide, we shall not stray,
The Divine whispers, 'Trust and stay.'

Each step we take, a purpose unfolds,
In trials faced, His love it holds.
With hearts entwined in sacred embrace,
We find our peace in His boundless grace.

Surging Forward in Spirit

With wings of faith, we rise anew,
In spirit fierce, we journey through.
Through storms that clash, and winds that moan,
The fire within cannot be outshone.

Each challenge met, a lesson learned,
In every heart, the passion burned.
Together we stand, in strength we grow,
Onward with love, in faith we sow.

Echoing Voices of Courage

In silence deep, courage calls loud,
With faith as our shield, we stand proud.
Each voice a beacon, together we rise,
In unity's strength, we are wise.

Through trials fierce, we shall not bend,
With hearts ablaze, on Him we depend.
Together our voices will shatter the night,
In echoing courage, we spread the light.

Testament of Tenacity

In the face of doubt, we hold the line,
With steadfast hearts, and spirits divine.
Each step forward, a testament true,
In trials united, we will break through.

Through whispered fears, we rise and stand,
With tenacity woven, hand in hand.
Faith fuels our quest, love paves our way,
In the dance of grace, we shall not sway.

The Divine Uplift

In the stillness, grace descends,
Heaven's whispers softly blend.
Hearts awakened, spirits rise,
Touched by love that never dies.

Hands uplifted, we reach wide,
In faith's embrace, we shall abide.
Guided by a radiant light,
Through the shadows, we take flight.

Strength in Silence

In quietude, our souls ignite,
Gentle echoes fill the night.
With patience found in sacred space,
We find our strength, our sacred place.

In moments still, the heart can hear,
The whispers of the Divine near.
Through trials faced, we learn to stand,
In silence, we reclaim our land.

Covenant of Resilience

Through storms that rage and tempests roar,
We hold each other, rich in lore.
Bound by promises of old,
In every strife, our hearts are bold.

With every tear, a seed is sown,
In faith's embrace, we're never alone.
Together, we rise and heal,
In love's embrace, we'll always feel.

Wings of Hope Unfurled

In the dawn, a light appears,
Dispelling doubt, dissolving fears.
With wounded hearts, we dare to dream,
On wings of hope, our spirits beam.

Through valleys low and mountains high,
With faith unyielding, we shall fly.
In every struggle, strength is found,
With open hearts, we soar unbound.

The Sacred Dance of Perseverance

In shadows deep, we find our way,
With faith as guide, we shall not sway.
Each step a pledge, a heart of gold,
Through trials faced, our story told.

With every fall, we rise anew,
In strength united, we break through.
In sacred circles, hands entwined,
In every heartbeat, love defined.

The journey long, yet beauty grows,
In every challenge, wisdom flows.
Together we dance, in sacred grace,
With every breath, we find our place.

Eternal Flame of Hope

Out of the darkness, a light appears,
A flicker of faith to calm our fears.
Through storms that rage, we keep it bright,
An eternal flame, our guiding light.

In silence speaks, the heart's pure wish,
A whispered prayer, a sacred swish.
When shadows linger, we lift our eyes,
To the starry skies, where love never dies.

Each moment cherished, like precious gold,
A story of courage, eternally told.
For in our hearts, the fire stays,
An eternal flame that never decays.

Harmony in Turmoil

In chaos loud, the soul finds peace,
A gentle whisper that brings release.
In brokenness, the beauty shines,
Harmony weaves through tangled lines.

Amidst the noise, we seek the song,
In unity, we can't go wrong.
With hearts aligned and spirits free,
We create a world where love can be.

For every storm that tries to bind,
A brighter dawn is sure to find.
In struggle's grip, we lift our voice,
Through turmoil's depths, we make our choice.

Awakening Light

In dawn's embrace, a new day breaks,
Awakening souls, the spirit wakes.
In moments quiet, we hear the call,
The light within ignites us all.

With every heartbeat, wisdom grows,
The path of truth, as love bestows.
Through eyes wide open, let us see,
The beauty in the tapestry.

In each small step, a journey starts,
The world transformed, with open hearts.
Awakening light, we rise and soar,
In unity's glow, forevermore.

The Light from Within

In the stillness of the night,
A whisper calls my name.
A spark ignites the soul,
A flame that sets me free.

Guided by faith's embrace,
I walk on paths of grace.
The light within me shines,
Illuminating dreams.

Covenant of the Brave

In shadows deep we stand,
United hearts in prayer.
With courage as our shield,
We rise beyond despair.

Each promise binds us tight,
In love we find our might.
For in the face of fear,
We choose the path that's right.

The Road Less Troubled

A winding road appears,
Where few have dared to tread.
With faith to guide my steps,
I walk where angels led.

Through trials I will grow,
In strength I shall abide.
Trusting in the journey,
With spirit as my guide.

Beyond the Veil of Mourning

In tears of loss we grieve,
Yet hope is never lost.
For love will find a way,
To bridge the final cost.

Beyond this earthly veil,
A promise waits in grace.
In light we shall embrace,
The souls we cannot trace.

Awakening From Shadows

In silence deep, the spirit wakes,
From weary dreams, the heart remakes.
A whisper calls through night so vast,
Embrace the light, release the past.

Shadows flee, as dawn appears,
Through trials faced, we've shed our fears.
With open hands and souls inspired,
We rise anew, with love desired.

The path ahead, though steep and long,
Is filled with hope, a sacred song.
In every step, divinity flows,
Awakening hearts, as truth bestows.

From ashes cold, the fire ignites,
With faith as guide, we seek the heights.
In unity, our voices blend,
Awakening grace, till journey's end.

Resilience of the Spirit

In trials faced, the spirit stands,
With hopeful eyes and steadfast hands.
Through storms that rage and winds that wail,
The heart persists, it shall not fail.

Each scar a mark of battles won,
In faith we find where we belong.
With every fall, we learn to rise,
In darkness, light within us lies.

Together, strong, we forge ahead,
With love as guide, no fears to dread.
The strength we yield, a sacred force,
Resilience found in love's true course.

In moments fierce, when hope seems lost,
The spirit thrives, no matter the cost.
For in the trials, wisdom speaks,
Resilience blooms where love's heart seeks.

Ascendancy of Faith

In valleys low, our spirits soar,
With whispers sweet, we seek for more.
Each step we take, a dance of grace,
Faith's gentle hand, our warm embrace.

Through shadows cast, the light reveals,
A path that time and love conceals.
With every breath, our souls unite,
In faith's embrace, we find our light.

Mountains high, and oceans wide,
In faith we trust, in love we bide.
No storm can shake the heart's firm hold,
Ascendancy of faith, purest gold.

Together we climb, through doubts and fears,
With faithful hearts, through all the years.
Each prayer a seed, in soil it sows,
Ascendancy comes, as true love grows.

The Lantern in the Dark

When shadows loom and visions fade,
A lantern glows, divine cascade.
It lights the way through darkest night,
Guiding our hearts to find the light.

With every flame, a story told,
Of love and hope, of courage bold.
In quiet moments, strength reveals,
The lantern's warmth, our soul it heals.

Through winding paths, where fears abide,
We carry forth, with faith as guide.
In unity, our spirits soar,
The lantern glows forevermore.

In times of doubt, when shadows fall,
The light remains, enduring all.
In every heart, we find a spark,
The lantern shines within the dark.

The Fortress of Belief

In shadows cast by doubt and fear,
The heart stands strong, a beacon clear.
On faith's foundation, we shall build,
A fortress where all hope is filled.

With prayer, we raise the sacred wall,
To guard our souls, lest they should fall.
In unity, our spirits blend,
A bond that time can never end.

The storms may rage, the tempests roar,
But in this haven, we restore.
For every trial shapes our trust,
In God, in love, in hope, we must.

With every tear, a lesson learned,
Through every trial, our hearts discerned.
Together, hand in hand we stand,
In the fortress built on faith's command.

A watchful eye upon us stays,
Guiding us through life's winding ways.
In reverence, we shall abide,
In the fortress, where love resides.

Blossoming in Adversity

In fields of sorrow, seeds are sown,
From cracks of hardship, courage grown.
Each petal shines with strength anew,
A testament to struggle true.

When shadows loom, we bend but stay,
From trials faced, we find our way.
Through darkest nights, a light we seek,
In whispered prayers, our souls grow strong and meek.

The thorns may prick, but still we rise,
With every breath, our spirits fly.
In pain, a beauty intertwined,
A sacred truth within we find.

For every storm that shakes our ground,
A blossom waits to be unbound.
In faith, we water our despair,
And nurture hope with loving care.

From ashes, flowers break the dawn,
In adversity, we are reborn.
With hearts aflame, we face the strife,
In blooming grace, we find our life.

Hymn of the Brave

Raise your voice, O hearts of fire,
In unity, we lift our choir.
For every battle fought and won,
We sing a song for everyone.

With courage steeped in love and light,
We stand as one to face the night.
In trials fierce, our spirits soar,
Bound by a faith that opens doors.

Each step we take on trembling ground,
With every heartbeat, hope is found.
The brave embrace their destiny,
In every struggle, we are free.

For in the depths of darkest days,
A hymn of strength our spirits raise.
In silence, whispers turn to song,
Together we are brave and strong.

So let us stand through thick and thin,
With hands outstretched, and spirits kin.
In every note, a glory shared,
An anthem bold for all who dared.

Transcendence Through Tribulation

In trials faced, the spirit soars,
Through pain's embrace, the heart restores.
With every wound, the soul ascends,
In suffering, a strength that mends.

The tempest strikes, yet still we stand,
With faith, we rise, a steadfast band.
In shadows cast, the light breaks through,
Transcendence found in all we do.

From ashes born, we gain our wings,
With trust in God, our spirit sings.
No mountain high can hold us back,
In tribulation, find the track.

With every tear, a blessing flows,
In every wound, a wisdom grows.
Through darkest nights, we seek the dawn,
Transcendence waits, and we move on.

For in the struggle lies our peace,
A journey grand where doubts release.
With every step, a path unveiled,
Through tribulation, we have sailed.

Serene After the Storm

In shadows deep, the storm did roar,
Yet faith did shine, through trials more.
The skies now clear, with peace restored,
We gather strength, in love's accord.

Each raindrop falls, a tear that's shed,
Yet blooms arise, from soil bred.
The heavens speak, with whispers sweet,
In quiet grace, we find our feet.

From chaos wrought, a harmony,
In every heart, there's unity.
With arms outstretched, we rise anew,
And walk in light, forever true.

Echoes of Endurance

In trials faced, the spirit grew,
Each step we took, our courage flew.
With every fall, we learned to rise,
In weary hearts, hope never dies.

The echoes call, from ages past,
With whispered tales, of love steadfast.
Through storms that rage and shadows cast,
Together bound, in peace amassed.

In strength we weave, a tapestry,
Of dreams fulfilled, and souls set free.
Our voices blend, a sacred song,
In harmony, we all belong.

Alchemy of the Heart

In silent prayer, the heart transforms,
From ash and dust, it finds new forms.
With every breath, a spark ignites,
Converting pain to inner lights.

The love we share, a golden thread,
In darkest nights, it brightly led.
What once was sorrow, forged in grace,
Through trials faced, we find our place.

In every loss, a lesson gleaned,
The soul refines, the heart redeemed.
Each moment lived, a chance to part,
The mundane veils the alchemy of the heart.

Heavenly Resilience

From heights above, the angels sing,
A melody of hope they bring.
Through valleys low, and mountains tall,
Their gentle hands, they lift us all.

The path is steep, with stones that bruise,
Yet through the pain, we shall not lose.
For in our souls, a fire burns bright,
Guiding us through the darkest night.

With every trial, we learn to stand,
With faith as strong, as ocean sand.
In harmony, we rise, we soar,
A testament, of love's great core.

Harmony After Tempest

In storms of doubt, our faith will shine,
Through darkest nights, His love aligns.
The tides may rage, yet hope will rise,
With gentle whispers, He calms the skies.

When thunder roars, and fears assail,
We seek the light, our hearts prevail.
A promise made, in grace we stand,
Together held, by His guiding hand.

The waters surge, but we are free,
In perfect peace, our souls shall be.
With every drop, a chance to grow,
In harmony's embrace, we reap what we sow.

Through trials faced, His strength we find,
In every heart, His love entwined.
We journey forth, with spirits bold,
In unity, our stories told.

Covenant of the Brave

Oath of valor, hearts aflame,
In darkest times, we seek His name.
With threads of courage, woven tight,
We stand as one, prepared to fight.

The trials faced, the battles waged,
In every soul, a fire is staged.
Together strong, we rise anew,
In faith and love, our bond will stay true.

With hands held high, we forge ahead,
On sacred ground, our spirits fed.
A covenant made, through trials and tears,
With hearts ablaze, we conquer our fears.

The path is steep, the night is long,
But in His light, we find our song.
For every step, a purpose clear,
In unity, we conquer fear.

Threads of Salvation

In woven strands, our lives entwine,
Each act of love, a sacred sign.
Through trials faced, through tears we shed,
With faith as thread, our spirits fed.

The fabric rich, with colors bright,
In darkest days, we seek the light.
Each moment shared, a testament,
To grace that flows, in hearts content.

With every stitch, His blessings flow,
In gentle hands, His love will grow.
In threads of hope, our lives are sewn,
In unity, we find our home.

The tapestry speaks, of grace divine,
With every heart, in His design.
Together strong, we are made whole,
In woven dreams, we find our goal.

The Celestial Promise

In skies above, a promise glows,
The stars aligned, where glory flows.
With every breath, the heavens sing,
A sacred vow, our hearts will bring.

The moonlit path, where shadows fade,
In quiet moments, His peace cascades.
A celestial bond, through time and space,
In every soul, we find His grace.

The dawn will break, new hope shall rise,
In every heart, He hears our cries.
With hands outstretched, we seek the way,
In faith we stand, come what may.

The promise kept, through every storm,
In trials faced, our hearts transform.
In love profound, we walk as one,
In celestial light, our spirits run.

Seraphic Ascension

Above the clouds, where angels sing,
In realms of light, a golden wing.
The grace of heaven, pure and bright,
Guides souls to realms of endless light.

In sacred air, where echoes dwell,
We seek the peace, the holy swell.
With fervent hearts, we lift our gaze,
To find the truth in love's sweet blaze.

Beneath the stars, the echoes soar,
Each whispered prayer, a sacred lore.
Through trials faced, our spirits rise,
As seraphs sing beyond the skies.

In unity, our voices blend,
The path of faith, a blessed mend.
With every step, the promise clear,
In seraphic love, we leave our fear.

Awake anew, with strength reborn,
In holy light, our hearts adorn.
Together bound, we journey high,
In seraphic grace, we shall rely.

The Heart's Sanctum

In quiet chambers, deep within,
A sacred space where love begins.
Through storms of doubt and waves of pain,
The heart's sanctum remains our gain.

With gentle whispers, souls unite,
In faith's embrace, we find the light.
Each tender thought, a prayer takes flight,
Within this haven, all feels right.

In trials faced, we gather near,
Through trust and hope, we conquer fear.
In gratitude, our spirits soar,
The heart's sanctum opens wide its door.

With every heartbeat, love's refrain,
In still communion, loss turns gain.
The sacred bond, forever strong,
In heart's sanctum, we all belong.

As dawn awakens, spirits gleam,
In unity, we chase the dream.
Together bound in sacred trust,
Our hearts aflame, our faith is just.

Sunlit Fortitude

In morning's light, we rise anew,
With sunlit strength, our spirits true.
Each golden ray, a promise bright,
In sunlit fortitude, we find our might.

With open hearts, we face the day,
Through trials fierce, we'll find our way.
In shadows cast, we stand as one,
Together bound, till the day is done.

The strength within, like rivers flow,
In faith and love, we bravely grow.
With courage fierce, we face the flame,
In sunlit fortitude, we stake our claim.

As storms arise, we shall not fade,
Our spirits bold, in love portrayed.
In unity, our journey's song,
Sunlit fortitude makes us strong.

With every dawn, we rise once more,
In faith renewed, we will explore.
With hearts ablaze, let courage show,
For in this light, our souls shall glow.

The Spirit's Reawakening

In slumber deep, the spirit waits,
For whispers soft to open gates.
In stillness found, the truth will spark,
The spirit's reawakening, ignites the dark.

With tender grace, the light breaks through,
In ancient songs, the soul renews.
Through trials faced and shadows cast,
The spirit's journey, free at last.

In sacred moments, silence speaks,
The heart's desire, the spirit seeks.
Through love unbound, we rise and shine,
In spirit's dance, we intertwine.

As dawn ascends, the shadows flee,
In unity, we find the key.
The spirit's flame, forever bright,
Illuminates the path of light.

Awake we stand, in love's embrace,
In every heart, we find our place.
Together strong, we break the chains,
With spirit free, eternal gains.

Faith's Unyielding Climb

In shadows deep, we journey forth,
With hearts ablaze, we seek the truth.
Each step we take, a sacred guide,
For in our faith, we shall abide.

Through trials fierce, our spirits rise,
With every tear, we lift our eyes.
For grace descends, a gentle balm,
In storms of doubt, we find our calm.

The mountain high, we dare to scale,
With whispered prayers, we shall prevail.
Each doubt we cast, a stone unchained,
In unity, our souls reclaimed.

The Ascendant Spirit

Awake, O soul, to realms above,
In light we dwell, in joy we move.
With wings of faith, we learn to fly,
Embracing hope, we touch the sky.

In every heart, a sacred flame,
An echo of the holy name.
Together bound, we rise anew,
A tapestry of love so true.

For every battle fought in grace,
We find the strength to seek His face.
In spirit's flight, we shall rejoice,
For love transcends, we hear His voice.

Embracing the Dawn

As daybreak shines on hills so bright,
We gather here, hearts full of light.
In morning's glow, our hopes unbind,
With hands entwined, our paths aligned.

The sun ascends, dispelling night,
In every shadow, faith ignites.
Each dawn a gift, a chance to start,
Renewed in strength, we share one heart.

With whispers soft, we greet the day,
In love's embrace, we find our way.
For every moment, blessings pour,
Together we shall rise and soar.

From Ashes We Soar

From ashes born, a spirit free,
We rise again, in unity.
With courage found, we break the chains,
In every loss, a love remains.

With faith as fire, we find our place,
In trials faced, we seek His grace.
From depths of sorrow, hope will bloom,
In mourning's veil, we find our room.

With each rebirth, we stand anew,
Our spirits soar, divinely true.
In light we dwell, in love we strive,
For from the ashes, we revive.

Blessed by Struggles

In shadows deep, we find our might,
Through trials faced, we see the light.
Each burden carried, a lesson learned,
In faith and hope, our spirits burned.

With every tear, a seed is sown,
From ashes rise, a heart reborn.
The path is rough, yet grace is near,
In struggle's grip, we shed our fear.

Embrace the pain, for joy shall bloom,
In darkest nights, dispel the gloom.
Each trial faced, a step to grace,
In faith's embrace, we find our place.

With every stumble, upward we climb,
Through stormy seas, we heal in time.
For in the challenges, strength appears,
Blessed by struggles, we conquer fears.

Pilgrimage of Perseverance

Upon this road, we tread anew,
With weary hearts, yet spirits true.
Each footstep taken, a prayer in song,
In unity, we all belong.

The winding path, it tests our will,
But faith within gives strength to fill.
Through valleys low and mountains high,
The soul ascends, prepared to fly.

In every challenge, wisdom gleams,
A guiding light, illuminating dreams.
For every stumble, a chance to rise,
In perseverance, true honor lies.

With every mile, our spirits soar,
In love's embrace, we seek for more.
The pilgrimage leads us, hand in hand,
Together we journey, forever we stand.

Wings of Divine Redemption

Upon the winds, our spirits take flight,
In grace and mercy, we find our light.
Each heart that's broken, a chance to mend,
With wings of love, our souls ascend.

Through trials faced, redemption gleams,
In whispered prayers, we've traced our dreams.
For every sorrow, a joy will bloom,
In divine embrace, we cast off gloom.

With faith as guide, we dare to soar,
O'er past mistakes, we close the door.
A second chance, a gift bestowed,
In love's presence, our spirits flowed.

Let burdens fall, let worries cease,
In endless grace, we find our peace.
With wings of mercy, we rise above,
In sacred journey, we know true love.

The Pathway to Renewal

In every dawn, a fresh start waits,
Through trials passed, we open gates.
With every breath, a chance to grow,
In nature's song, our spirits flow.

The pathway winds through light and shade,
In gentle whispers, we hear His aid.
With open hearts, we seek the truth,
In life's embrace, we find our youth.

For every ending, a new beginning,
In love and grace, our lives are spinning.
Through seasons change, we stand renewed,
In sacred moments, our souls imbued.

With every step, we weave His plan,
A journey shared, hand in hand.
On this path, divine and clear,
To renewal's grace, we draw so near.

The Manifest Melodies of Triumph

In shadows deep, faith starts to rise,
A whisper soft, beneath the skies.
With every step, a heart reborn,
The soul ignites, a new dawn's morn.

Through trials faced, our spirits soar,
Each note of courage, a sacred core.
In harmony, we find our way,
Guided by light, through night and day.

With hands uplifted, we praise the dawn,
For every tear, a strength withdrawn.
In each embrace of grace divine,
We stand united, your will, our sign.

So sing we now, in joy and peace,
Let troubles fade, their grip release.
With voices joined, a glorious hymn,
The love of faith, our lifeblood's brim.

Thus manifest, our triumph clear,
In every heartbeat, you draw near.
Together, hand in hand, we stand,
Our spirits bright, at your command.

From Trials to Triumph

In valleys low, where shadows breed,
We walk in faith, fulfill the need.
With every challenge, hope ignites,
And lifts us up to wondrous heights.

Our hearts aflame with steadfast trust,
Through pain and fear, we rise from dust.
Each trial faced, a lesson learned,
In darkest nights, the flame we've turned.

The path is steep, but light shall guide,
With each small step, our souls abide.
From ashes rise, like phoenix flight,
Embracing warmth of morning bright.

For every storm, there comes a calm,
In whispered prayers, we find the balm.
Through faith's embrace, we break the chain,
And dance upon the fields of grain.

From trials faced, we soar anew,
In unity, our spirits grew.
With every breath, we claim the prize,
From grief to joy, our souls will rise.

Stepping Stones of the Spirit

Each stone we step, a tale of grace,
In our journey, we find our place.
With faith as guide, we walk along,
The path of love, a sacred song.

From every stumble, strength unfolds,
In quiet moments, the truth it holds.
With every crack, a seed of light,
Awakens hope in darkest night.

The whispers soft, like breezes flow,
In the heart's chambers, love will grow.
As stepping stones lead us through strife,
Transforming pain into new life.

Together we climb, hand in hand,
In unity, we take our stand.
With faith's embrace, our spirits soar,
To heights unknown, forevermore.

So tread these stones with open hearts,
For each is blessed, and never parts.
In every step, a promise true,
Stepping stones direct us to you.

The Quiet Power of Belief

In silence deep, the soul takes flight,
With every prayer, a spark of light.
Through faith's embrace, our spirits learn,
In quietude, the heart will yearn.

For when the world seems cold and gray,
A whisper calls, it shows the way.
In stillness found, the truth will bloom,
And chase away the shadows' gloom.

The power lies in soft refrain,
With every hope, we break the chain.
Each thought of love, so freely cast,
Builds bridges strong, and binds us fast.

In moments still, our hearts align,
With every breath, your light will shine.
Through trials faced, let courage swell,
In quiet power, we find our well.

So let us trust, in what we feel,
In the gentle hush, our strength is real.
With each belief, we are set free,
In quiet power, we find the key.

Sacred Steps of Resilience

In the valley of shadows, we walk,
Faith guides our feet with tender grace.
Through trials we rise, steadfast we talk,
With hearts ignited, we embrace.

Each stumble whispers lessons profound,
In silence, the spirit starts to soar.
With every heartbeat, hope is found,
In unity, we open the door.

The storms may roar, the skies may darken,
Yet in our hearts, a beacon shines.
Together we stand, unbroken, aarken,
In the sacred winds, our faith aligns.

As dawn breaks forth, the light cascades,
Renewed with purpose, we bravely tread.
With sacred steps, our journey invades,
A tapestry of love, softly spread.

Resilience blooms like flowers rare,
In each soft petal, strength we see.
With gratitude, we lift our prayer,
In sacred steps, we're forever free.

Manifestation of the Soul's Strength

In the whispers of night, dreams take flight,
The soul's strength shines, a radiant glow.
Through valleys low and mountains high,
We gather the courage to grow.

In every heartbeat, power resides,
With intention pure, we manifest.
In silence, the universe abides,
Revealing paths where we are blessed.

With every breath, creation begins,
Moments of magic, ever near.
In the dance of life, our spirit spins,
Embracing love, casting out fear.

Through trials faced, our essence blooms,
A garden nourished by faith's warm light.
With open hearts, dispelling glooms,
We rise again, hearts burning bright.

Manifest your dreams with fervent trust,
Each thought a seed in the soil of time.
In the garden of hope, love is a must,
The soul's strength sings, a cherished rhyme.

Faith's Everlasting Flame

In the depth of night, a flame flickers,
Faith's warmth ignites the darkest hour.
With whispered prayers, our hearts grow thicker,
In its glow, we find our power.

Through trials faced, as storms arise,
This flame within will never wane.
In every tear, a new sunrise,
Faith endures through joy and pain.

The whispers of hope, they guide our way,
With every step, the flame grows bright.
Through shadows cast, we find the day,
In faith's embrace, we claim our light.

When doubts assail and fears collide,
The flame within will not depart.
With courage fierce, we stand beside,
In faith's embrace, we heal the heart.

Everlasting flame, our souls unite,
In its embrace, we journey on.
Through every battle, in darkest night,
Faith remains as dusk meets dawn.

Emblems of Endurance

In the tapestry of life, we weave,
Threads of courage that bind us strong.
Through trials faced and love we give,
We stand as one, where we belong.

Each scar a story, each wound a tale,
Of strength found in the darkest test.
In every falter, we shall prevail,
In unity, we know we're blessed.

An emblem worn upon the heart,
With every challenge, we bloom anew.
Through storms and strife, we'll never part,
In every sunrise, we find our view.

In faith, we flourish like the dawn,
Resilient souls, a shining race.
Through every dusk, we carry on,
Emblems of endurance, we embrace.

Together we rise, hand in hand,
A chorus of hope in every song.
With love as our guide, we take a stand,
In emblems of endurance, we are strong.

The Revered Rebound

In valleys deep, where shadows dwell,
The spirit cries, a whispered bell.
From ashes rise, with faith anew,
The heart restored, in light imbued.

Through trials faced, and burdens borne,
In quiet prayer, the soul reborn.
Each setback leads to lessons learned,
From darkened paths, the spirit turned.

With every tear, a seed is sown,
In love's embrace, we're never alone.
The strength within, our guiding light,
A cherished bond, through day and night.

As rivers flow, the heart does mend,
In sacred trust, our spirits blend.
Revered we stand, together strong,
In unity, we find our song.

The journey shared, so richly blessed,
In faith and hope, we find our rest.
With every heartbeat, love will abide,
In the revered, our souls unite.

A Journey Through the Shadows

In twilight's grasp, the lost often roam,
Yet deep in darkness, we find our home.
With whispered prayers and lanterns bright,
We seek the dawn to guide our flight.

Steps falter on this winding road,
Yet strength appears to lighten the load.
Each shadow cast holds lessons dear,
In trust, we face our deepest fear.

The sorrows faced, like tempest's breath,
Reveal the grace found near to death.
Through trials harsh, the spirit learns,
To rise again, as the heart yearns.

In moments dim, the light breaks through,
A glimpse of hope, in steadfast view.
Together we stand, united as one,
Through shadows dark, a new day's begun.

With faith as compass, we journey on,
Through vale of tears, till fears are gone.
For in the depths, where shadows play,
We find our strength to light the way.

Tempest to Tranquility

Amidst the storm, where fears abound,
The raging tides, no peace is found.
Yet in the chaos, hearts can soar,
Through faith restored, we shall explore.

With every wave, a lesson learned,
In fervent prayer, the spirit turned.
When lightning strikes, and thunder rolls,
The stillness waits to calm our souls.

From tempest's wrath, the calm shall rise,
The sun breaks forth, revealing skies.
In nature's dance, we find our path,
Through storms endured, we feel love's wrath.

With gentle grace, the waters still,
In peace we find the heart's true will.
Through trials faced, we stand in light,
From tempest's fear, to tranquil night.

For every storm that clouds the day,
A promise waits to lead the way.
In harmony, we find the key,
From tempest wild, to serenity.

The Ascension of Hope

Upon the hills, where dreams take flight,
The dawn embraces, all bathed in light.
With every heartbeat, hope ascends,
A journey bold that never ends.

Through valleys low, where shadows creep,
In faith we climb, and never sleep.
Each step we take, a sacred trust,
In love we rise, as we must.

With open arms, the sky unfolds,
A tapestry of stories told.
In unity, our spirits soar,
The whispers speak of something more.

The trials faced, a distant past,
In hope reborn, a light so vast.
Together bound, we chase the dream,
In every heart, a radiant beam.

The ascension calls, we heed the voice,
In every choice, the heart must rejoice.
For in the light, our path is clear,
The ascent of hope, forever near.

The Dance of the Determined

In solemn prayer, they gather near,
With whispered hopes that conquer fear.
Their hearts entwined in sacred trust,
For faith endures, it turns to dust.

Through trials faced, they sing their song,
In unity, they grow more strong.
Each step they take, a vow they make,
In light of love, their path awake.

In shadows cast, the light breaks through,
A dance of souls, both brave and true.
With every twirl, they rise once more,
Together bound, they seek what's pure.

In every heartbeat, grace descends,
True purpose found, the spirit mends.
With lifted hands, they reach the skies,
In perfect rhythm, they shall rise.

With every step, they shake the ground,
Where hope resides, and peace is found.
Their dance, a promise, ever bold,
In faith's embrace, their story told.

Grace Ascendant

In dawn's embrace, the light reveals,
A gentle strength that hope conceals.
With every breath, a chance to grow,
In grace's flow, all hearts will know.

Through valleys deep, and mountains high,
Their spirit soars, a bird in sky.
With trust in love, they stand so tall,
In quiet grace, they'll never fall.

The trials faced, they sharpened minds,
In every challenge, wisdom finds.
With open arms, they greet the day,
In grace ascendant, they shall stay.

Each humble heart, a sacred flame,
In unity, they're all the same.
With song of joy, they make a bond,
In love's embrace, forever fond.

Ascend they shall, to heights divine,
In fervent hope, their souls align.
With faith ignited, paths unfold,
In grace ascendant, brave and bold.

Revelations at the Summit

Atop the peak, where stillness reigns,
The heart unlocks, and truth remains.
In whispered winds, the secrets flow,
Revelations bloom, the spirit grows.

The wider view reveals the past,
In every shadow, lessons cast.
With each sunrise, new eyes behold,
In sight of grace, the brave and bold.

With open minds, they seek the light,
In every breath, the endless fight.
The journey made, through thick and thin,
In every struggle, strength begins.

In sacred stillness, voices ring,
The song of truth, a sacred spring.
With humbled hearts, they stand in awe,
Revelations drawn, they hear the law.

As mountains bow to skies above,
Each click of time, a gift of love.
In unity, they find their peace,
Revelations shared, the soul's increase.

Climbing the Mountain of Faith

With every step, the heart prepares,
A journey marked by love and cares.
Through winding paths, and rocky trails,
The spirit soars, the courage trails.

Together strong, they lift each other,
Like sister, friend, or holy mother.
In faith they trust, through stormy skies,
With eyes on truth, their spirits rise.

The summit calls, a sight so grand,
In unity, they take their stand.
With hands entwined, they heed the call,
Climbing higher, they shall not fall.

In gentle whispers, hope ignites,
Through darkest hours, they seek the lights.
With every prayer, a bond is made,
In faith's ascent, they won't evade.

Atop the peak, where visions blend,
The mountain's grace, they will commend.
With souls ablaze, they mark the day,
Climbing the mountain, come what may.

Holy Resilience

In shadows deep, we seek the light,
With faith as our shield, we stand in might.
Through storms of doubt, our spirits soar,
In holy strength, we rise and more.

Each trial faced, a blessing found,
In whispered prayers, our hope unbound.
With steadfast hearts, we journey on,
In sacred grace, our fears are gone.

Embrace the path, though rocky and steep,
In trusting love, our souls we keep.
With every step, we find our way,
In holy resilience, come what may.

Through laughter shared and sorrows shared,
In every moment, we felt cared.
Divine assurance, a guiding star,
In sacred bonds, we heal the scar.

Let not the trials lead us astray,
For with each dawn, we see the day.
In holy resilience, we shall thrive,
Through battles fought, we stay alive.

The Sacred Arc of Striving

In the quiet hours of morning's grace,
We lift our hearts to a sacred place.
With dreams in hand, we take the leap,
In the arc of striving, our souls we keep.

With every step, the journey unfolds,
A story written in the stars, retold.
Through trials faced, our spirits gain,
In seeking truth, we conquer pain.

With faith ablaze, we rise each day,
In love's embrace, we find our way.
The sacred arc, a whisper sweet,
For in our striving, our souls repeat.

Through valleys low and mountains high,
In every tear, a reason why.
The sacred dance of hope and strife,
In every moment, we find our life.

Together we stand, with hearts aligned,
In unity, our strength defined.
With every breath, we lift our plea,
In the sacred arc, we are set free.

Petition of the Perseverant

In the hush of night, our voices rise,
A petition spoken, beneath the skies.
With hearts aflame, we seek the grace,
Of divine presence in this place.

Through trials faced, we find our way,
In steadfast hope, we choose to stay.
The strength within, like rivers flow,
In perseverance, our spirits grow.

With hands united, we raise our song,
In the dance of faith, we shall be strong.
For every challenge, a chance to rise,
In our petition, no compromise.

With loving kindness, we lift each prayer,
In gratitude, our burdens bear.
Through darkest times, we find the light,
With every step, we fight the fight.

So let us share this sacred plea,
In unity's strength, we shall be free.
Petition of the perseverant heart,
Together we stand, never apart.

The Divine Echo of Strength

In whispered winds, we hear a call,
A divine echo that guides us all.
With each heartbeat, strength we embrace,
In the dance of life, we find our place.

Through trials faced, we build our might,
In every shadow, we seek the light.
The echo resonates in every soul,
In love's embrace, we are made whole.

With faith unshaken, we rise anew,
In every struggle, a clearer view.
The divine echo, a song of hope,
In unity's grace, we learn to cope.

Through mountains high and valleys deep,
The strength within, our promise to keep.
In echoes that speak of courage found,
Together we stand, our hearts unbound.

So heed the call, and let us sing,
The divine echo of every thing.
With every voice, a harmony,
In strength united, we shall be free.

From Ashes to Glory

From ashes we rise to the light,
In faith, we soar to the height.
The trials we face, a sacred test,
With every struggle, our hearts are blessed.

In darkness, a whisper calls near,
A promise of hope, dispelling fear.
Each step we take on the path so bright,
Is guided by love, our eternal light.

Through storms we wander, yet find our way,
With grace in our hearts, we shall not sway.
The past may haunt, but it does not bind,
In the strength of our spirit, true peace we find.

From ashes to glory, our journey unfolds,
With faith as our anchor, and vision that holds.
Together we rise, hand in hand we stand,
In the promise of life, we'll forever expand.

Embrace the fire that fuels your soul,
Let love be your guide, make broken hearts whole.
From ashes to glory, the story we write,
Is one of redemption, forever in light.

The Rebirth of the Soul

In shadows we wander, seeking the dawn,
A whisper of grace, where hope is reborn.
With every tear shed, the soul learns to heal,
In the depths of despair, love teaches us real.

A gentle embrace from the heavens above,
The reinvention of spirit, the power of love.
As petals unfold from a fragile bloom,
The rebirth of life breaks the chains of the gloom.

Awake from the slumber, arise and believe,
The strength within you, a gift to receive.
Each moment a chance to grow and renew,
In the circle of life, we're forever made new.

With courage we face each trial along,
In unity's heartbeat, we gather our song.
The rebirth of the soul, a journey profound,
In the arms of the divine, true solace is found.

Together we rise, let the spirit take flight,
Embracing the day, transforming the night.
The soul's gentle rebirth, in faith we revolve,
As love guides our hearts, and together we evolve.

Embers of Hope

In the quiet of night, where darkness reigns,
Embers of hope flicker, despite the pains.
A spark in the silence, a light in the gloom,
Reminding us all that new life will bloom.

Through trials and shadows, we carry our dreams,
In the heart of the storm, the light still gleams.
With courage we stand, united in grace,
The embers of hope, in every embrace.

Though wearied and worn, our spirits ignite,
In the warmth of each other, we find the light.
Each deed of kindness, a flame drawn anew,
In the tapestry woven, hope carries us through.

With every heartbeat, our prayers take flight,
Counting blessings anew in the soft morning light.
Embers of hope whisper tales of the brave,
In the depth of our struggle, we learn how to save.

So let us remember, in unity's call,
The embers of hope shine brighter for all.
With love as our guide, we shall never despair,
For in the heart of the faithful, hope lingers there.

In the Embrace of Grace

In the embrace of grace, our hearts find rest,
With gentle reminders, we are truly blessed.
Through trials and triumphs, we walk side by side,
In the warmth of connection, our spirits abide.

With each passing moment, a gift to unwrap,
In the stillness of being, we rest in His lap.
The burdens we carry, transformed into light,
In the embrace of grace, we rise to new heights.

The journey of faith, a winding road,
In laughter and tears, together we strode.
With love as our compass, our burdens grow small,
In the embrace of grace, we find strength for all.

Each soul is a vessel, a beacon that shines,
Reflecting the beauty of love's sacred designs.
In the embrace of grace, we learn to be free,
Together we flourish, in unity's decree.

So let us rejoice in this beautiful space,
For life is a treasure, a divine embrace.
In the embrace of grace, we're forever entwined,
In the heart of creation, true peace we will find.

Harvesting Courage

In fields of fear, we stand so tall,
With hope as our guide, we shall not fall.
Through storms and trials, we sow with grace,
In the heart of struggle, we find our place.

Each seed of strength, in soil of tears,
Grows brighter with faith, dispelling our fears.
Together we reap what love has sown,
With courage as our shield, we are not alone.

The sun will rise on paths once dim,
We lift our voices in grateful hymn.
In unity, we harvest our might,
The bond of our spirits ignites the night.

So, let us gather, let the world see,
In courage, together, we shall be free.
For every trial is merely a chance,
To harvest the strength found in our dance.

Through every shadow, a blessing may bloom,
In hearts entwined, dispelling all gloom.
We are the courage, the light and the flame,
In a world of fear, we triumph in His name.

Sanctity of the Unbroken

In silence, we gather, hearts pure and wide,
Bearing the scars of the storms we bide.
Each crack, a story, each flaw, a grace,
In the sanctity of love, we find our place.

With every burden, we rise to defend,
The beauty of life that will never bend.
In faith, we embrace the pieces we hold,
For in brokenness, our truth is told.

A tapestry woven, both rough and smooth,
By hands that are tender, we find our groove.
In moments of prayer, our spirits align,
In sacred whispers, divinity shines.

Let not the world dim the light within,
For unbroken souls will always begin.
With hope as the anchor, we sail the sea,
In the sanctity found, we are truly free.

Together we'd stand, unyielding and bold,
With stories entwined, like threads of gold.
In the embrace of kindness, our spirits ascend,
In the sanctity of the unbroken, we mend.

Veils of Despair Lifted

When shadows linger and hope seems thin,
We lift our eyes to the light within.
With faith as our lantern, we walk the way,
Veils of despair slowly fade away.

In moments of doubt, we gather our might,
For dawn breaks forth after long, starless night.
With every prayer, a new flame ignites,
Guiding us forth to the heights of the lights.

Tenderly woven, our hearts beat as one,
Together we rise toward the shining sun.
In the warmth of love, we cast off the shroud,
Veils of despair crumble, and we speak loud.

Let the winds of hope carry us high,
With wings of the Spirit, we'll soar through the sky.
In unity clasped, we find our reprieve,
The veils of despair, in grace, we believe.

So, lift up your voice, let your spirit sing,
In the face of darkness, we're destined to spring.
For hope is our vision, and love is our flame,
In the depths of our souls, we rise without shame.

In the Hands of Providence

In the quiet moments, we find our way,
Held gently by fate, come what may.
With every heartbeat, a purpose unfolds,
In the hands of Providence, our story is told.

When trials surround us, we shall not fear,
For love guides our steps, drawing us near.
With grace as our armor, we journey on,
In the hands of Providence, we are reborn.

Each twist and turn, a divine design,
Within every challenge, blessings align.
Through valleys of shadows, we walk with light,
In the hands of Providence, our spirits take flight.

So let us surrender to paths not our own,
For in every struggle, love's seeds are sown.
With eyes toward heaven, we trust and believe,
In the hands of Providence, we'll surely receive.

Let the whispers of grace guide us each day,
In the dance of existence, we'll find our way.
For destiny cradles the souls that it calls,
In the hands of Providence, love never falls.

Echoing the Divine Whisper

In the silence where shadows blend,
The gentle voice begins to send,
A call that resonates within,
Awakening calm from where we've been.

Listen closely, it calls your name,
In love's embrace, we find no shame,
Through trials faced and lessons learned,
In every heart, the truth discerned.

Beneath the stars, a sacred space,
Where grace and mercy interlace,
Each prayer a bird that takes its flight,
In sacred night or morning light.

The whispers guide like morning dew,
In every moment, we find what's true,
With every beat, our spirits soar,
Connected deeply, forevermore.

Let the echoes of love resound,
In every soul, a holy ground,
With faith as our unbroken chain,
We'll find our peace, in joy or pain.

Safe in Surrender

In the stillness, we learn to trust,
Be still my heart, adjust to dust,
Let go the weight we hold so tight,
In surrender, we see the light.

With open hands, we give our fears,
Release the doubts, dissolve the tears,
In every heartbeat, find the grace,
Embrace the love that we all chase.

In the depth of stormy seas,
A calm awaits, we breathe with ease,
Unfolding wings where spirits fly,
In sacred peace, we learn to sigh.

Each step in faith, a gentle plea,
In trust we walk, for we are free,
The path is clear, though shadows loom,
In surrender, we bloom in bloom.

Safe in the arms of the divine,
Every moment, your light will shine,
With every breath, let hope arise,
For in surrender, true freedom lies.

The Soul's Concord

In harmony where spirits meet,
Echoes of love pull us from defeat,
Tuning hearts to nature's song,
Together we rise, where we belong.

In gentle whispers, unity grows,
The pulse of life, in silence flows,
Each soul a thread, a vibrant ray,
Woven together, night and day.

Through trials faced and burdens shared,
The warmth of faith will keep us paired,
We embrace the light, the joy so bright,
In every moment, we're shining light.

With open arms, we gather near,
Embracing all, dissolving fear,
In kindness found, our spirits cheer,
Together, love is always clear.

The soul's concord, a sacred bond,
A journey shared, a love beyond,
In every heartbeat, we will find,
Divine connection, heart entwined.

Awakening Joy

In the dawn of a brand new day,
We find our heart in light's array,
With every breath, the spirit sings,
Awakening joy that freely springs.

From shadowed valleys to mountain high,
In nature's arms, our worries die,
Embracing love, we heed the call,
In joy's embrace, we rise, we fall.

With laughter bright as morning's grace,
In sacred moments, we find our place,
Together singing in joyful praise,
Life's sweet wonders, our hearts will raise.

In the dance of life, we twirl and sway,
Finding blessings in each foray,
With open hearts and hands wide bare,
Awakening joy, beyond compare.

So let us spread the light we know,
In every act, let kindness flow,
For in our joy, the world will see,
The beauty of love, eternally.

The Blessing of Struggles

In shadows deep we often roam,
Through trials vast, we seek our home.
Each burden lifts our spirits high,
In strife, we learn to touch the sky.

The storms may rage, the winds may howl,
Yet in our hearts, we hear Thy cowl.
For in the dark, Thy light will shine,
A path ahead, forever divine.

With every tear, a lesson sewn,
In pain, a seed of faith has grown.
Through fiery trials, we find our way,
To brighter dawns, a new today.

The struggle bends, but does not break,
In every fall, new strength we take.
With courage firm, we shall ascend,
For in all things, we find our Friend.

So let us greet each fleeting day,
With hearts ablaze, we humbly pray.
In every challenge, grace we find,
The blessings of our souls aligned.

Grace in the Hardest Trials

When valleys low weigh on our soul,
In faith, we trust, we still feel whole.
For in our struggles, grace does bloom,
Transforming darkness into room.

Each challenge faced is but a test,
A call to rise, to seek the best.
In trials harsh, we're not alone,
Thy gentle whispers guide us home.

Through every whisper of despair,
Thy love, O Lord, is always there.
In brokenness, we find the way,
To brighter skies another day.

With lifted hearts, we face the storm,
In every tear, Thy peace is born.
A power deep, within us lies,
In hardest trials, our spirit flies.

So let us walk with steadfast grace,
Through every shadow, seek Thy face.
Together, hand in hand, we strive,
In every pain, our hope's alive.

Ascension of the Heart

From depths below, we rise anew,
With every beat, we seek what's true.
In moments still, our spirits soar,
To realms of love forevermore.

The burdens we with patience bear,
With open hearts, we offer prayer.
Each longing whisper leads us near,
To sacred realms, where skies are clear.

In every trial, strength is born,
A sacred gift in each new dawn.
Ascension waits for those who strive,
In faith and hope, we come alive.

Through valleys dark, the light will shine,
In love's embrace, our hearts entwine.
With every step, we feel Thy grace,
In divine love, we find our place.

So let us lift our voices high,
With joyful hearts, reach for the sky.
In unity, we rise and rise,
As one, we soar, beyond the skies.

The Path to Renewal

Upon the road of life we tread,
Through twists and turns, we forge ahead.
In every step, a chance to grow,
The seeds of hope begin to sow.

For every loss that we may face,
Brings forth a chance to feel Thy grace.
With open hearts, we search and seek,
In moments weak, Thy love we speak.

Transformation comes from deepest pain,
As rain revives the verdant plain.
In trials faced, we find what's true,
Our paths reborn in morning dew.

So let us walk with heads held high,
Embrace the storms, and touch the sky.
For every end brings forth a start,
In every sorrow, a healing heart.

With faith unwavering, we then stand,
Together, guided by Thy hand.
In life's great dance, we find our way,
The path to renewal starts today.

Light Through the Cracks

In shadows deep, the grace does seep,
A gentle beam where souls may weep.
Through weary hearts, the rifts shall glow,
With whispered truths that guide us slow.

Beneath the weight of strife we stand,
Held by the warmth of the Maker's hand.
Each crack reveals a story bright,
Of hope reborn, of purest light.

The dawn awakens weary eyes,
To see the world unveil its ties.
In every flaw, a lesson speaks,
In faith and love, our spirit peaks.

Though storms may rage and winds may howl,
We find our strength, on faith we prowl.
For light will spill, through darkest seams,
And guide us forth, into our dreams.

The Journey Towards Light

With every step on sacred ground,
The echoes of the past resound.
In search of truth, our hearts align,
Through valleys dim, to sun that shines.

The path is long, yet spirits rise,
Through trials faced, the soul complies.
On wings of prayer, we soar so high,
With fervent hopes that never die.

Each soul a flicker, a spark divine,
In unity, we intertwine.
Together we shall find our way,
To brighter dawns, a new-born day.

The journey winds through pain and grace,
Yet in our hearts, we find our place.
For every shadow hides a chance,
To dance with light, to sing and prance.

Faith's Unfaltering Road

Through winding ways, where doubts may creep,
We tread on faith, a promise deep.
With every trial, our hearts grow bold,
In whispered prayers, His love we hold.

The road may twist, the path obscure,
Yet in His light, our souls endure.
With steadfast hearts and minds aligned,
We walk the road, His truth enshrined.

In shadows cast, in valleys low,
We find the grace that leads us slow.
Each step we take brings us anew,
To faith's embrace, our hearts imbue.

For in this quest, we seek the flame,
That burns within, a holy name.
With every breath, we rise above,
On faith's unfaltering road, through love.

Divinity in the Struggle

In battles fought, where spirits clash,
Amidst the tears, the heart does thrash.
Yet through the pain, the light is near,
In every wound, the grace appears.

For every struggle bears a seed,
In trials faced, we find our creed.
With every burden, every sigh,
Divinity whispers, 'You shall fly.'

We rise from ashes, dust, and tears,
Transcending doubt, dismissing fears.
In hardships faced, we find our call,
To stand in light, to never fall.

The struggle etched upon our skin,
A testament to strength within.
Through every tear that we have shed,
In faith we walk, where angels tread.

Reverence in Rebirth

In the dawn of new light, we arise,
A whisper of grace in the skies.
From ashes of sorrow, we bloom,
Our spirits awakened, dispelling the gloom.

With each sacred breath, we transcend,
A cycle of life, no beginning, no end.
Through trials and tears, we find our place,
In the arms of the Divine, we discover His grace.

Nature sings softly, a hymn of the soul,
Guiding us gently, making us whole.
In the garden of faith, we sow our seeds,
Harvesting love as the spirit leads.

Time carves the path we must tread,
With reverence for those who have led.
In shadows of old, new hope we find,
A testament of love, eternally intertwined.

Through the trials faced, we forge our way,
With hearts unyielding, we choose to pray.
In unity strong, we gather as one,
A tapestry woven, forever begun.

Ascending Beyond Shadows

When darkness surrounds, we shall rise,
With faith like a beacon, piercing the skies.
Each step forward, we banish despair,
In the warmth of His love, no burdens we bear.

In the quiet of night, our spirits unite,
Casting away fears, embracing the light.
Through valleys of doubt, we journey along,
On wings of the spirit, we learn to be strong.

Mountains may tower, yet we shall not yield,
For the heart's gentle whisper is our shield.
Together we climb, through trials we grow,
In the garden of faith, His blessings we sow.

Life's winds may rage, but peace we shall claim,
In the call of the sacred, we honor His name.
In the echoes of silence, His promise we hear,
Ascend ever higher, without doubt or fear.

The shadows may linger, but hope shines bright,
We walk in the warmth of love's holy light.
Each hand that we hold, a strength to behold,
In the tapestry woven, our stories unfold.

The Spirit's Resurgence

Awaken, O soul, from slumber so deep,
In the journey of life, our promises keep.
A tempest may rise, but we stand tall,
With courage as armor, we answer the call.

The spirit ignites in moments of grace,
In trials we bear, we find our space.
With faith as our guide, we walk hand in hand,
United in purpose, together we stand.

From trials to triumphs, our voices sing,
The melody of life, in glory, we bring.
In the depths of our hearts, His love lights our way,
A lantern of hope, through night and through day.

As petals unfurl in the warmth of the sun,
We blossom together, our journey begun.
With each gentle breeze, the spirit takes flight,
In the essence of love, we find our true might.

From ashes we rise, a phoenix reborn,
In the promise of dawn, our spirits adorn.
With sacred resilience, we dance through the strife,
Embracing the journey, the miracle of life.

Serenity in the Storm

When the tempest rages and the thunder rolls,
In the heart of the chaos, the spirit consoles.
A prayer in our hearts, a light from within,
In the eye of the storm, we steadfastly grin.

Raindrops like blessings, they nourish the earth,
In the storms of our trials, we find our true worth.
As lightning may flash, we're guided by grace,
In the depths of the struggles, we find our embrace.

Through turbulent skies, our hearts become free,
In the chaos of life, we find harmony.
With faith as our anchor, we weather the gales,
In the promise of peace, our spirit prevails.

The winds may howl, yet we harbor no fear,
In the face of the storm, we draw ever near.
With love all around us, we shine like a star,
In the tempest of trials, we've come from so far.

When the clouds begin parting and sunlight breaks,
In the warmth of His love, our spirit awakes.
With gratitude and grace, our souls will transform,
Finding serenity deep in the storm.

The Climb to the Celestial

In shadows deep, the path does wind,
With faith as light, our hearts aligned.
Each step we take, a holy guide,
Toward the heights where hopes abide.

Upward we strive, the summit near,
Each whispered prayer, a fervent cheer.
A sacred promise, a guiding star,
In trials faced, we learn just who we are.

The burdens weigh, yet still we rise,
The spirit lifts, and fear defies.
Through light and darkness, we ascend,
For love divine will never end.

In the embrace of the endless sky,
Our souls ignite, as we comply.
Each breath, a pledge to seek and find,
The grace that binds all humankind.

On this journey, we walk as one,
With hearts ablaze beneath the sun.
In unity, we shall prevail,
The climb to joy, a holy tale.

Unyielding in Devotion

With steadfast hearts, we tread the way,
In prayerful hope, our spirits sway.
Each moment spent in sacred trust,
Through trials fierce, we know we must.

Fingers interlaced in grace,
A shared resolve, in this embrace.
Through storm and calm, our vow remains,
In every joy, in every pain.

The sacred bond, it holds us tight,
As shadows fall, we find the light.
In silence deep, our whispers rise,
A chorus sweet, that never dies.

In humble acts, our love is shown,
In giving hearts, we are not lone.
Each kindness sown, a seed divine,
Together, in faith, our lives entwine.

Forever strong, we face the fray,
United in spirit, come what may.
With arms uplifted, we shall sing,
A hymn of hope, to Him we bring.

Triumph Through Trials

Through darkest nights, the dawn will break,
In every struggle, hearts awake.
When hope seems lost, we find our way,
A beacon shines, to light our day.

The road is rough, but onward stand,
With open hearts, we take His hand.
Each step we face, a test of will,
In moments fraught, our faith to fill.

The mountain looms, yet we ascend,
With each hard-fought step, we shall mend.
In battles fought, and scars embraced,
Our spirits rise, our fears displaced.

Through trials tough, we grow anew,
In every tear, His love breaks through.
A story told, of strength regained,
In trials faced, true grace obtained.

With voices strong, we sing as one,
In triumph's glow, our race is run.
Life's symphony, a sacred song,
In love's embrace, we all belong.

The Soul's Resurrection

From ashes rise, the spirit pure,
In faith's embrace, we are secure.
Each loss we bear, a lesson learned,
Through valleys low, our souls are turned.

With broken wings, we seek the skies,
In every fall, the heart will rise.
From depths of sorrow, joy will bloom,
In darkness found, there shines no gloom.

The light within, it flickers bright,
Through shadows cast, it sparks the night.
In every heart, a sacred flame,
To rise again, we call His name.

In resurrection, hope restored,
With open arms, we face the Lord.
This journey leads from death to life,
In love's embrace, we end the strife.

So let us soar, on winds of grace,
With every breath, we find our place.
The soul reborn, it knows no end,
In love divine, we all transcend.

Revelations of the Resilient

In shadows deep, the soul does rise,
With faith as fuel, it pierces skies.
Each trial faced, a lesson learned,
In every heart, resilience burned.

From ashes cold, the spirit springs,
Embracing hope, on fragile wings.
A whisper soft, it calls us near,
In darkest night, the light is clear.

Bound by grace, we stand in awe,
A testament of love's own law.
Through storms we march, side by side,
In unity, our hearts abide.

With hands outstretched, we weave the fate,
In sacred bonds, we congregate.
Together strong, we face the fire,
Our spirits soar, we will not tire.

So let us sing, with voices loud,
In every heart, a vibrant crowd.
For in our story, truth prevails,
And through the struggle, love avails.

Sanctity of the Struggle

In trials faced, our spirits find,
The sacred path that leads the blind.
Each burden born, a chance to grow,
The warmth of grace begins to show.

Through hardship's gate, a lesson blooms,
In darkest hour, new life resumes.
The strength within, a guiding light,
That pierces through the thickest night.

When courage wanes, and hope feels lost,
We bear the weight, and count the cost.
In every scar, a story told,
The sanctity of souls so bold.

With gentle hands, we lift each care,
And in the struggle, love we share.
Transcending pain, we choose to climb,
To heal the wounds, embrace the time.

Together bound, in faith we grow,
Our hearts become the steady flow.
In patience held, our spirits rise,
The sanctity, a sweet disguise.

The Climb Towards Grace

Each step we take, though steep it seems,
Is woven tight with sacred dreams.
In every struggle, in every fight,
We inch towards the endless light.

The mountains high, they call our names,
In whispers soft, igniting flames.
With hearts ablaze, we journey forth,
Embracing pain, for what it's worth.

One foot in front, in rhythm found,
We lift our gaze from hallowed ground.
Through trials long, we push and strive,
In struggle's grip, we feel alive.

The summit shines, a dream embraced,
A testament to love and grace.
In unity, our burdens shared,
Each soul uplifted, deeply cared.

So let us climb, with hearts set free,
Embracing all that's meant to be.
With faith our guide, we'll find our way,
Towards grace divine, come what may.

Harmony in the Chaos

Amidst the storm, a silence sings,
In hearts of grace, the spirit clings.
Through raging tides, we find our peace,
A whispered prayer, will never cease.

In chaos found, a dance unfolds,
The beauty shines, in stories told.
With every tear, a seed is sown,
The harmony of hearts outgrown.

We walk the line, 'twixt light and shade,
In unity, our fears will fade.
Together bound, we face the thrill,
In sacred trust, our hearts we fill.

Each note we play, through dark and bright,
Creates a song, a shared delight.
In chaos deep, we'll find our song,
For in the struggle, we belong.

So let us dance, through disarray,
In every breath, we find our way.
For in this chaos, love will stay,
A harmony that leads the way.

Pilgrimage of the Soul

In the desert of doubt, I tread my way,
Seeking whispers of truth to guide my sway.
With each step forward, I shed my old skin,
In the stillness of spirit, my journey begins.

Through valleys of shadow, I rise and I fall,
In prayer and in silence, I hear the call.
Mountains may tremble, yet I shall not fear,
For the path of the righteous is always made clear.

With angels beside me, I walk in the light,
Carrying hope like a lantern so bright.
Harmony sings in the soft morning breeze,
As faith anchors me like the roots of the trees.

From ashes of doubt, my spirit takes flight,
Embracing the promise of dawn's early light.
In the pilgrimage deep within my core,
I find that my soul is forevermore.

Joy rises within as I reach for the sky,
With every heartbeat, I know I can fly.
On this sacred journey, I am made whole,
In the pilgrimage tender of my wandering soul.

The Light After Darkness

In shadows I wandered, lost in despair,
The weight of my burdens too heavy to bear.
Yet a flicker of hope began to ignite,
Whispers of promise danced in the night.

Through storms I have traveled, with heart torn asunder,
In silence I listened to the sound of thunder.
But the dawn broke gently, with warmth on my face,
Revealing the glory of infinite grace.

The chains of my past fell away like the mist,
As I reached for the heavens, in prayer I persisted.
Each tear turned to gold as I learned to forgive,
In the light after darkness, my spirit will live.

With every sunrise, I rise from the grave,
Transforming my sorrow, my heart becomes brave.
The road may be winding, but I shall not roam,
For in faith's tender glow, I have found my home.

So let the light lead me, I'll follow its path,
In the glow of compassion, I'll escape the wrath.
With courage and love, I stand in the grace,
For the light shines eternally in this sacred place.

Unbroken Chains of Faith

In moments of doubt, my heart seeks the way,
Through trials and troubles, I choose to pray.
Each chain that could bind me is forged in my trust,
In the power of faith, unyielding and just.

For the storms may be fierce, the shadows may loom,
Yet I find my strength in the light of the room.
With whispers of hope echoing through the night,
I gather my courage, and I choose the fight.

Together we stand, our spirits entwined,
Linked by devotion, our purpose aligned.
No distance can break what the heart has embraced,
For love is the bond that cannot be erased.

As we journey through valleys, and climb every hill,
With God as our anchor, we conquer with will.
The chains that unite us are unbroken and whole,
In the tapestry woven of each faithful soul.

In the whispers of night, together we rise,
With hearts intertwined, we reach for the skies.
Knowing with each step, we fulfill our fate,
In the unbroken chains of our love and faith.

Echoes of the Eternal

In the quiet of prayer, my soul starts to soar,
With echoes of wisdom that whisper once more.
Time dances lightly; it bends and it sways,
In the heart of the moment, eternity plays.

Each heartbeat resounds like a song from above,
The threads of existence weave tales of love.
In the depth of the silence, I'm drawn ever near,
To the chorus of grace that rings crystal clear.

Memories flood in like a river so wide,
Carried by currents of faith and of pride.
The essence of life flows like a stream through the soul,
In the echoes of ages, we find ourselves whole.

From the ashes of struggle to heights yet unseen,
The spirit, unyielding, remains evergreen.
With every reflection, I glimpse the divine,
In the cycle of life, the stars brightly shine.

So let the echoes guide, as I wander this earth,
Through valleys of blessing, and moments of worth.
In the tapestry woven with love from above,
I listen and learn in the echoes of love.

Tides of Transformation

Beneath the waves, the spirit churns,
With every tide, a new life learns.
Casting away burdens, the soul must soar,
In each ebb and flow, we find the door.

The moon whispers softly to the sea,
Guiding the hearts that long to be free.
Through storms and calm, the journey unfolds,
In the depths of the ocean, a treasure untold.

In shadows of darkness, the light breaks through,
Awakening dreams that are ancient and true.
With every dawn, hope rekindles the fire,
Transforming the spirit, lifting us higher.

Embrace the change, let the heart expand,
In each moment, find the divine hand.
For in surrender, we find our grace,
In the tides of transformation, we find our place.

So let us rise with the morning sun,
In unity together, our journey begun.
For every wave that crashes ashore,
Brings forth a promise, a chance to restore.

Heartbeat in the Struggle

In the silence of night, a heartbeat resounds,
Echoing strength where faith abounds.
Through each trial, we learn to endure,
In the clutches of darkness, our spirits secure.

The path may be rugged, with thorns intertwined,
Yet every stumble teaches the mind.
Let the burden not break us, but shape our design,
In the crucible of life, our souls brightly shine.

Each tear that we shed, a prayer in disguise,
An offering humble, we reach for the skies.
For every struggle, a lesson bestowed,
In the heartbeat of life, our true selves unfold.

With courage as armor, we rise from the dust,
In the grace of our hope, we learn to trust.
For the journey ahead is etched in our dreams,
In the heartbeat of struggle, our spirit redeems.

So let us tremble not in the face of the storm,
For through trials, we find where we are reborn.
United in strength, let our voices unite,
In the heartbeat of struggle, we illuminate the night.

The Call to Endeavor

Awake, O spirit! The time has come near,
To answer the call and shed every fear.
With hope in our hearts, let us venture wide,
For the path of endeavor is our sacred guide.

With faith as our beacon, and courage our way,
We gather the strength to seize the new day.
Through trials and journeys, our purpose refined,
In the bonds of our labor, true love we find.

The mountains may rise, and valleys may fall,
Yet the spirit of service shall beckon us all.
For each hand that reaches adds light to the fray,
In the call to endeavor, we find our way.

So let us arise, with vision aligned,
In the unity of action, our hearts intertwined.
With each step we take, let our voices sing,
In the call to endeavor, new hope we bring.

With passion as fuel, let our hearts ignite,
In the dance of creation, we trust in the light.
For the journey is sacred, our spirits set free,
In the call to endeavor, we are one, you and me.

When Hope Takes Flight

In the stillness of dawn, a whisper is born,
A glimmer of light as the shadows are worn.
With wings made of dreams, we rise up and soar,
In the heart of our being, hope opens the door.

With each vibrant color, the horizon awaits,
Embracing the change that our future creates.
In the tapestry woven from love and from strife,
When hope takes its flight, we embrace our life.

As branches are swayed by the gentle spring breeze,
Our spirits awaken, we flow with such ease.
With laughter and tears, the journey unfolds,
When hope takes its flight, our story is told.

So let us uplift each other in grace,
Embracing the beauty that all hearts embrace.
For in unity, we rise to the height,
When hope takes its flight, we bask in the light.

Together we'll wander where dreams intertwine,
In the chorus of creation, our souls will align.
With courage to follow, our spirits ignite,
In the moment of freedom, when hope takes flight.

The Vigil of the Valiant

In shadows deep, they stand aligned,
With faith as shield, their hearts entwined.
The whispers of the night call forth,
The brave arise, for what it's worth.

Their gazes fixed on stars so bright,
They seek the path to heaven's light.
In silence strong, their spirits soar,
With courage found, they fear no more.

Through trials faced, they hold their ground,
In unity, their strength is found.
With every prayer, they journey on,
The vigil kept till break of dawn.

Remembered souls, in peace they dwell,
And share their tales, their truths to tell.
For in the dark, a spark ignites,
The valiant rise, embracing sights.

So let the night be witness true,
To hearts that dare, to spirits new.
In hope and love, they take their stand,
The valiant ones, in God's own hand.

Ascending into the Light

From valleys low, to mountaintops,
The soul ascends, the journey hops.
With every step upon the way,
They find the strength to rise and pray.

The dawn awakens, casting gold,
A promise of the stories told.
Each breath a gift, each moment blessed,
In the pursuit, they find their rest.

With lifted hands, they praise the skies,
In gratitude, their spirit flies.
For in the climb, they shed their fears,
And wash their souls in holy tears.

The light descends, envelops all,
In unity, they heed the call.
A symphony of hearts combined,
Together forged, forever bind.

Ascending high, they touch the grace,
Embracing love, they find their place.
In every soul, a spark so bright,
Together forged, ascending light.

The Sacred Quest of the Soul

In every heart, a journey stirs,
To seek the truth as life occurs.
Through winding paths, both dark and bright,
The sacred quest ignites the light.

With humble steps, the seekers roam,
In search of peace, they wander home.
They gather strength from every scar,
In each reflection, guiding star.

The whispers call from ancient trees,
In every rustle, spirit frees.
Their souls entwined, they share the road,
In wisdom found, a shared abode.

Surrendering to love's embrace,
The sacred quest, a holy grace.
With open hearts, through trials faced,
The treasures found will not be replaced.

And when the journey meets its close,
They find the truth within, and rose.
The sacred quest, forever whole,
In every step, the journey's soul.

Resilience in the Heart of Prayer

In whispered words, the faithful speak,
With open hearts, they softly seek.
A resilience born in quiet grace,
In every tear, divine embrace.

The storm may rage, the earth may shake,
Yet in their chest, the heart won't break.
For in the prayer, a refuge stays,
A light emerging through the haze.

Connected souls, they lift their voice,
In harmony, they find their choice.
Through moments dark, they rise anew,
With faith that holds them, old and true.

With every thought, they weave a thread,
In unity, the spirit's fed.
Resilience found where hope prevails,
In every prayer, their strength unveils.

So let the heart in prayer abound,
In whispered hopes, their peace is found.
Resilience blooms, a sacred art,
In every soul, a fervent heart.